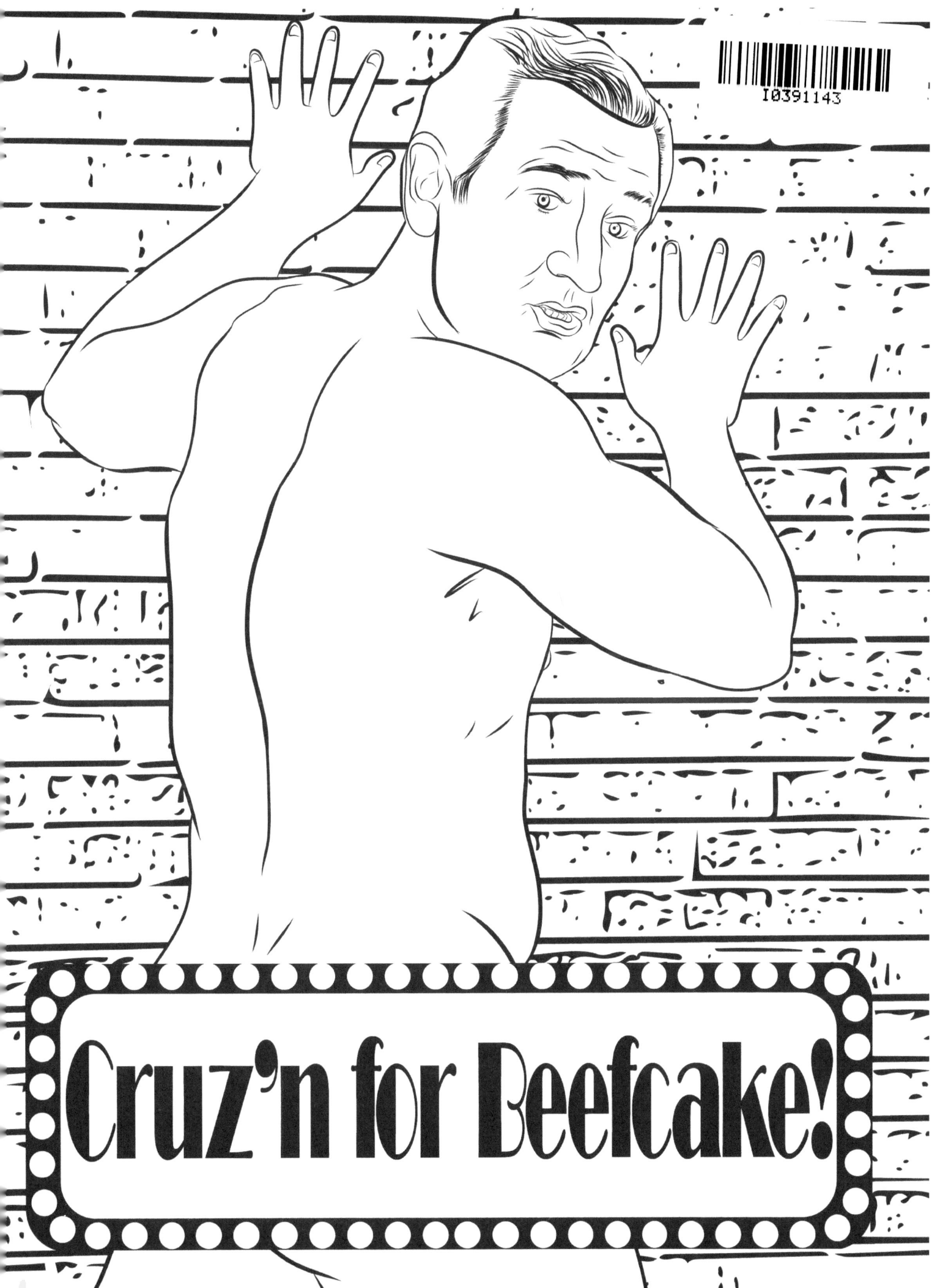

For more shenanigans

Tumblr: rocketship-ace
Instagram: rocketship.ace
Twitter: @rocketship_ace
Facebook: rocketship.ace.graphics
Teespring:

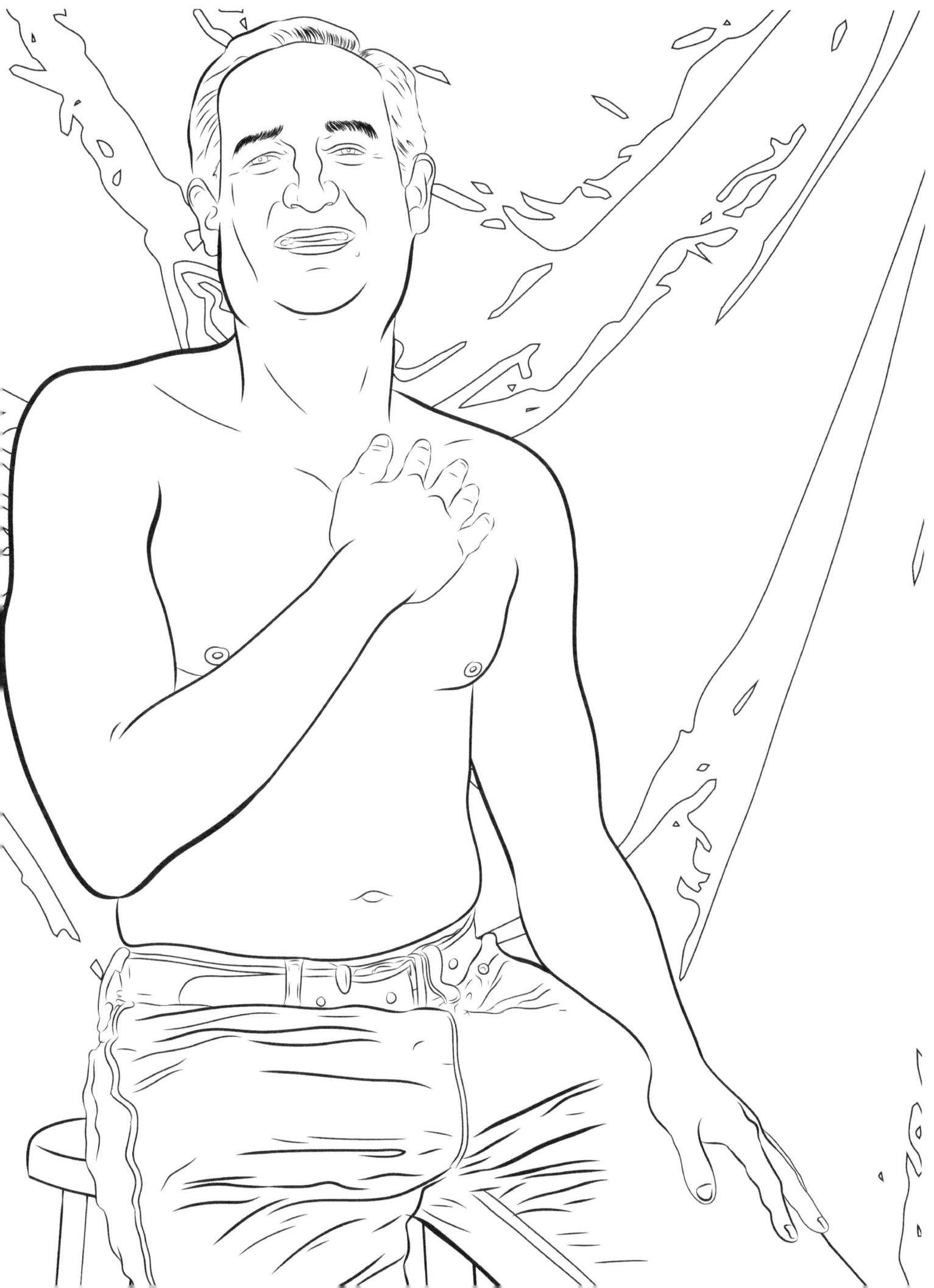

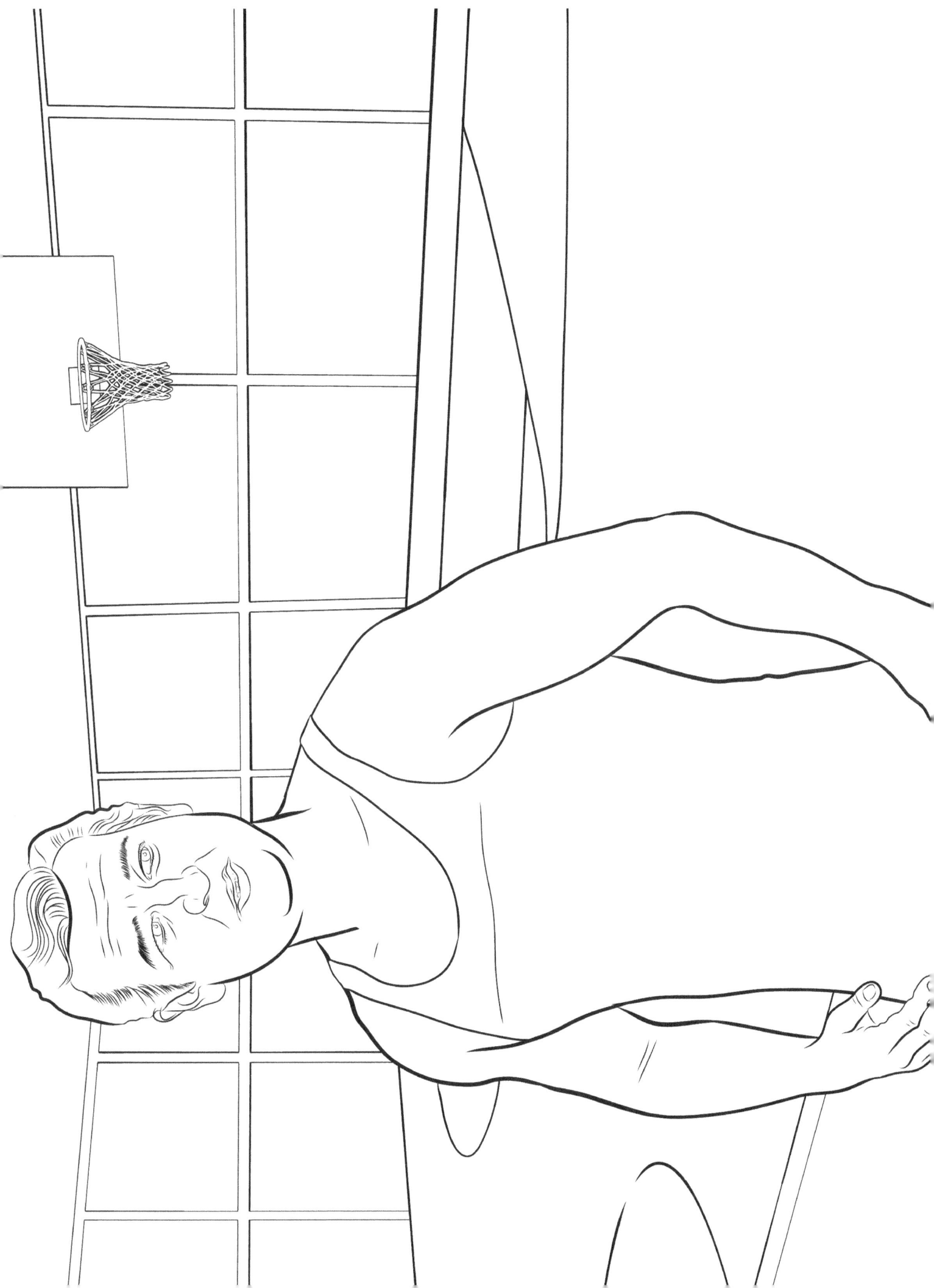

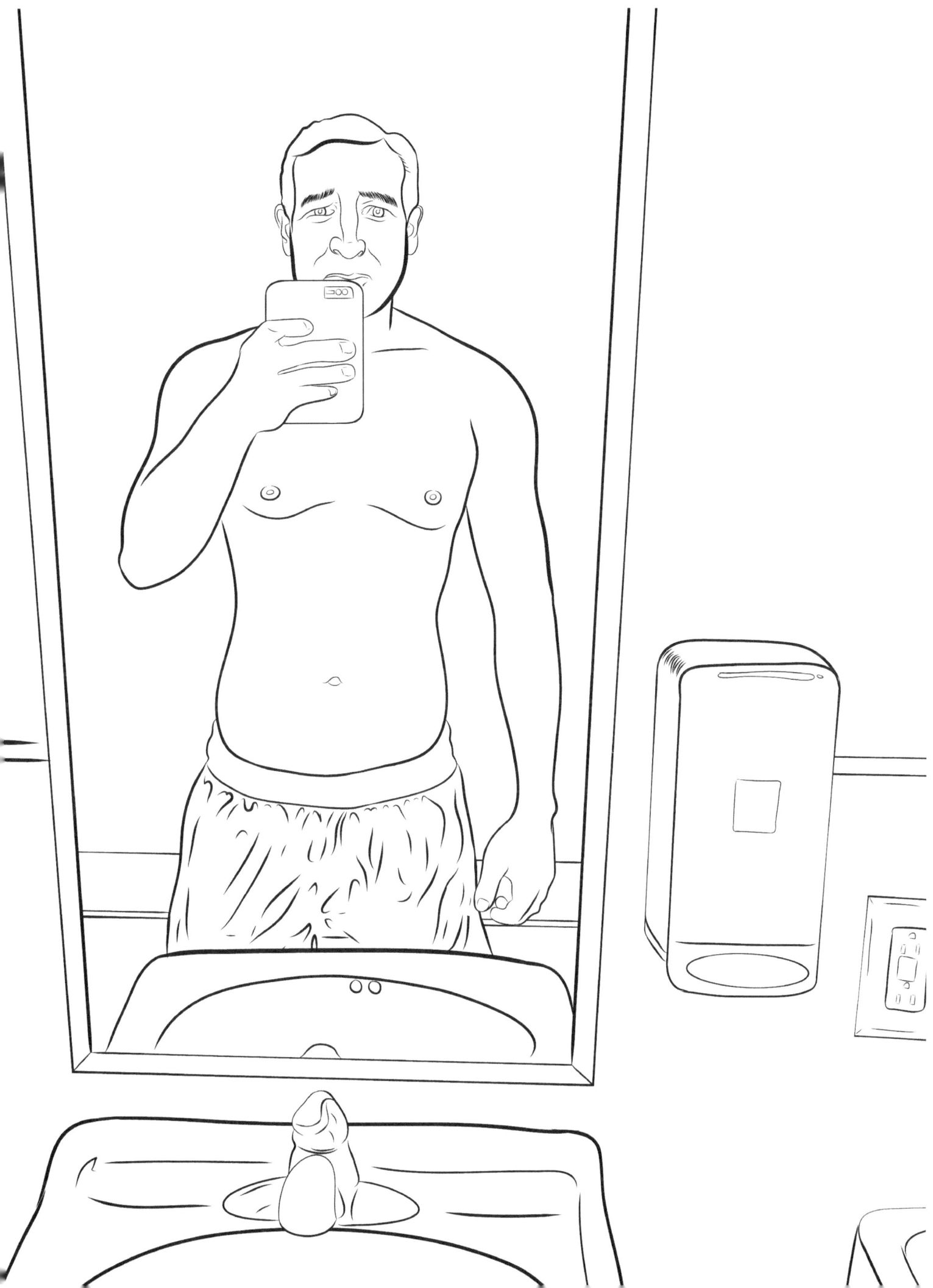

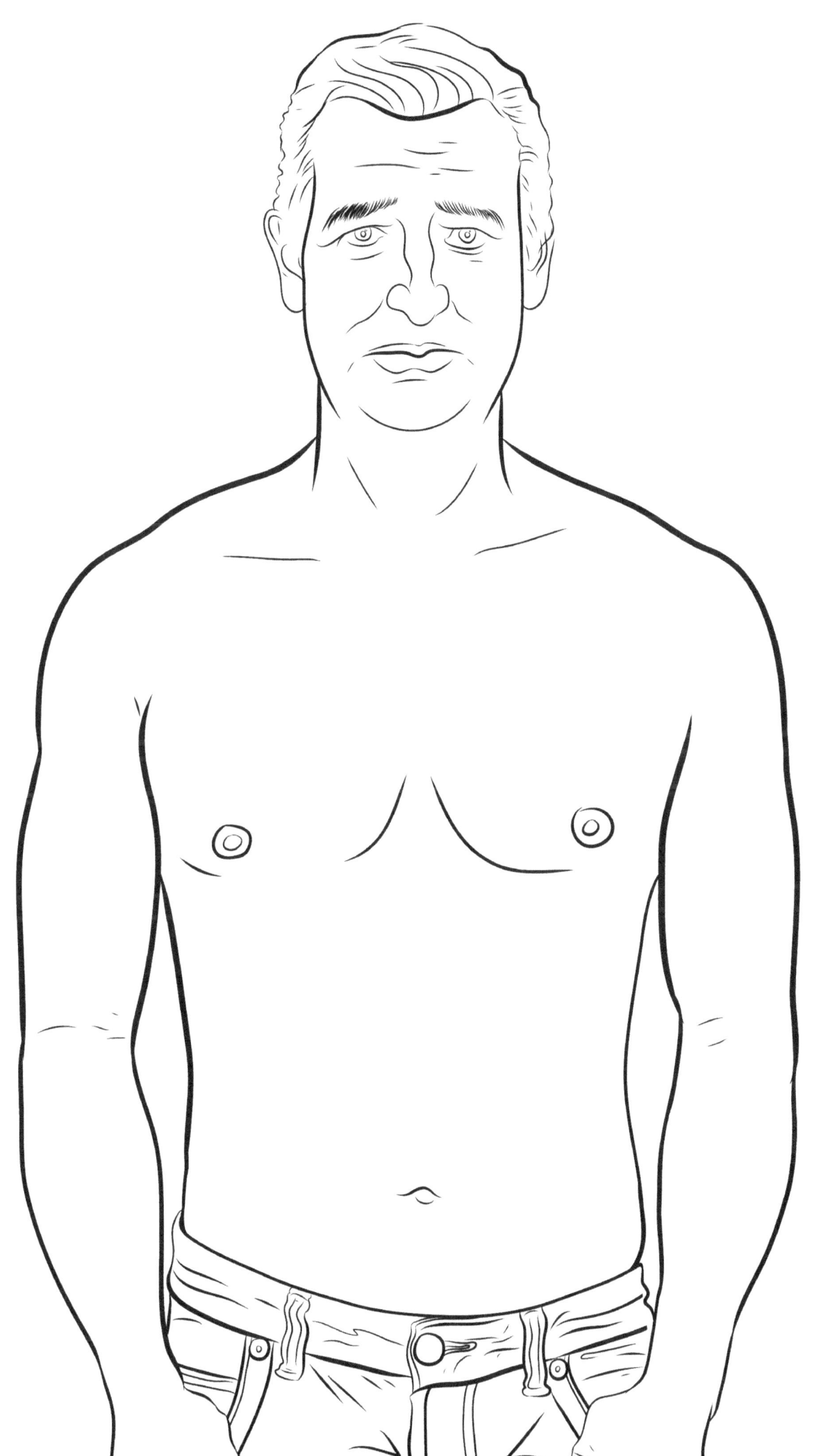

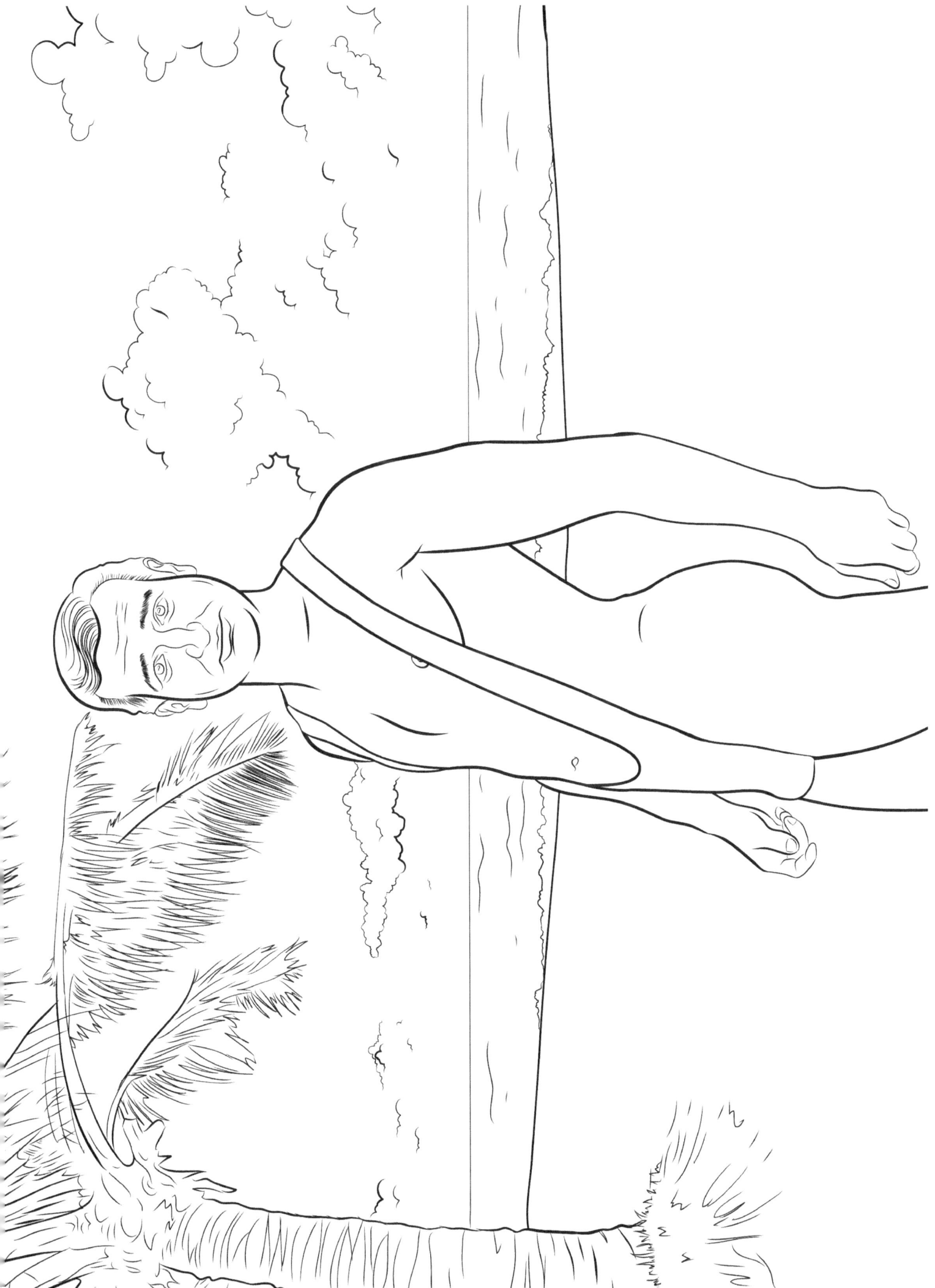

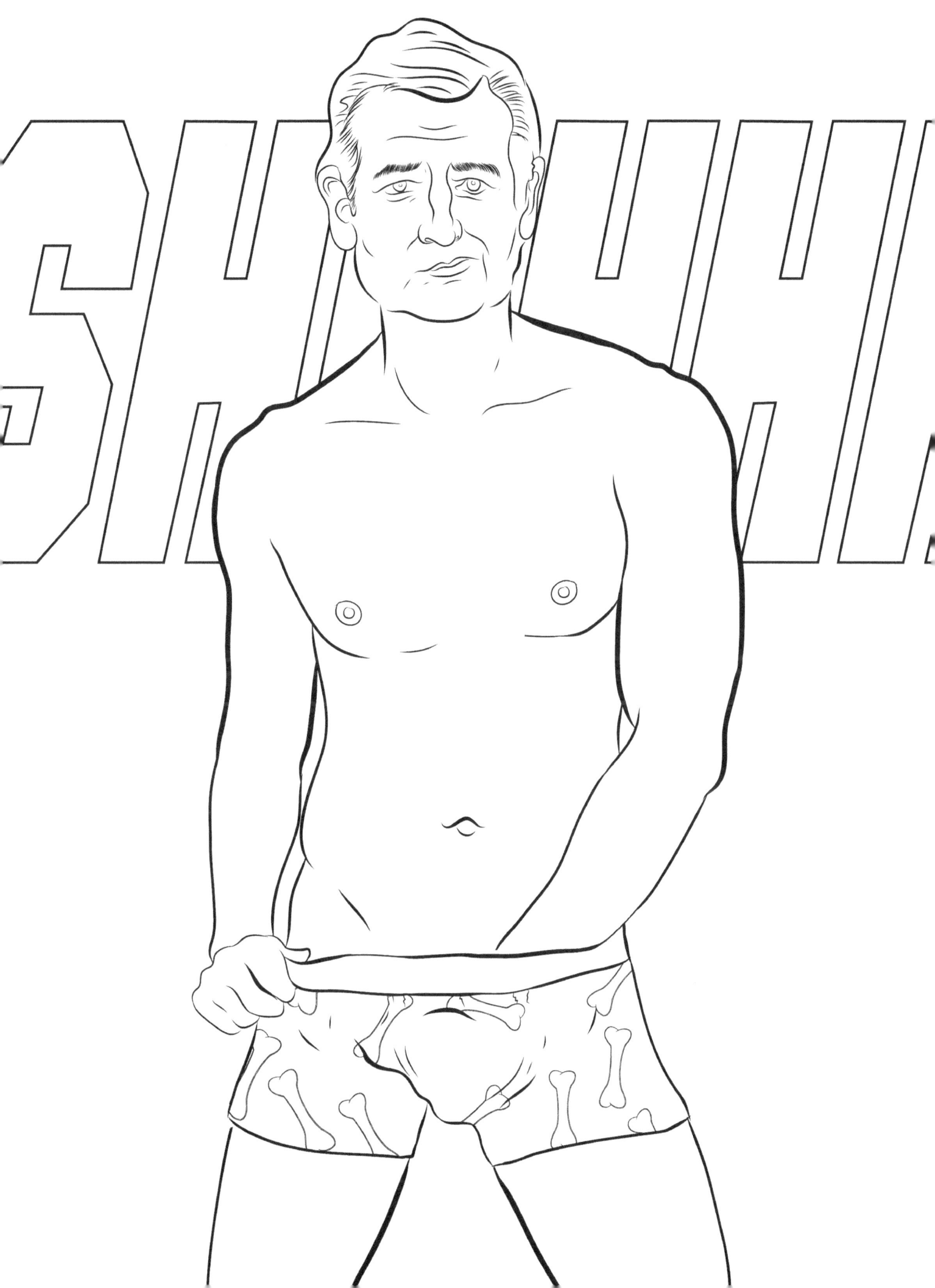

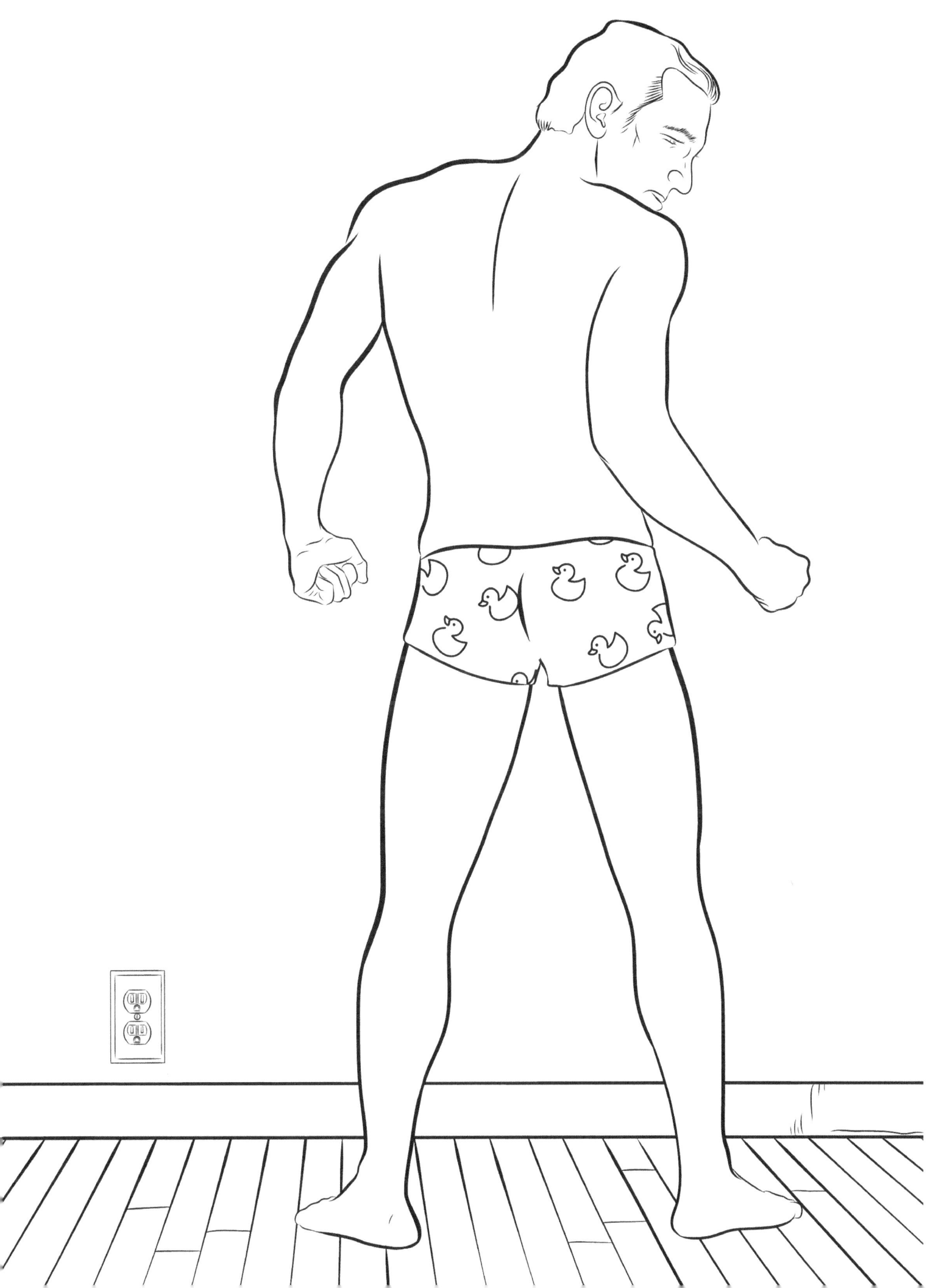

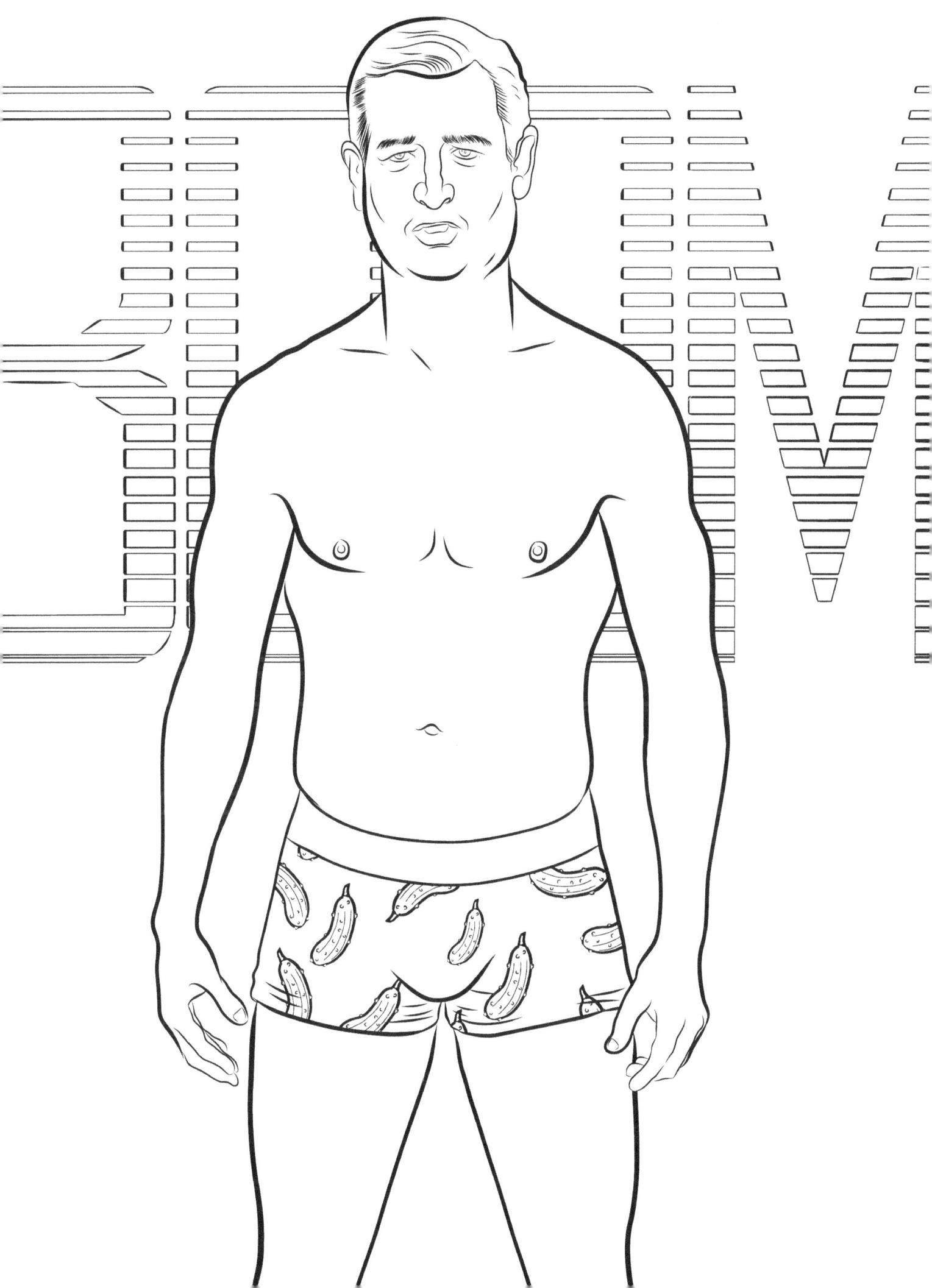

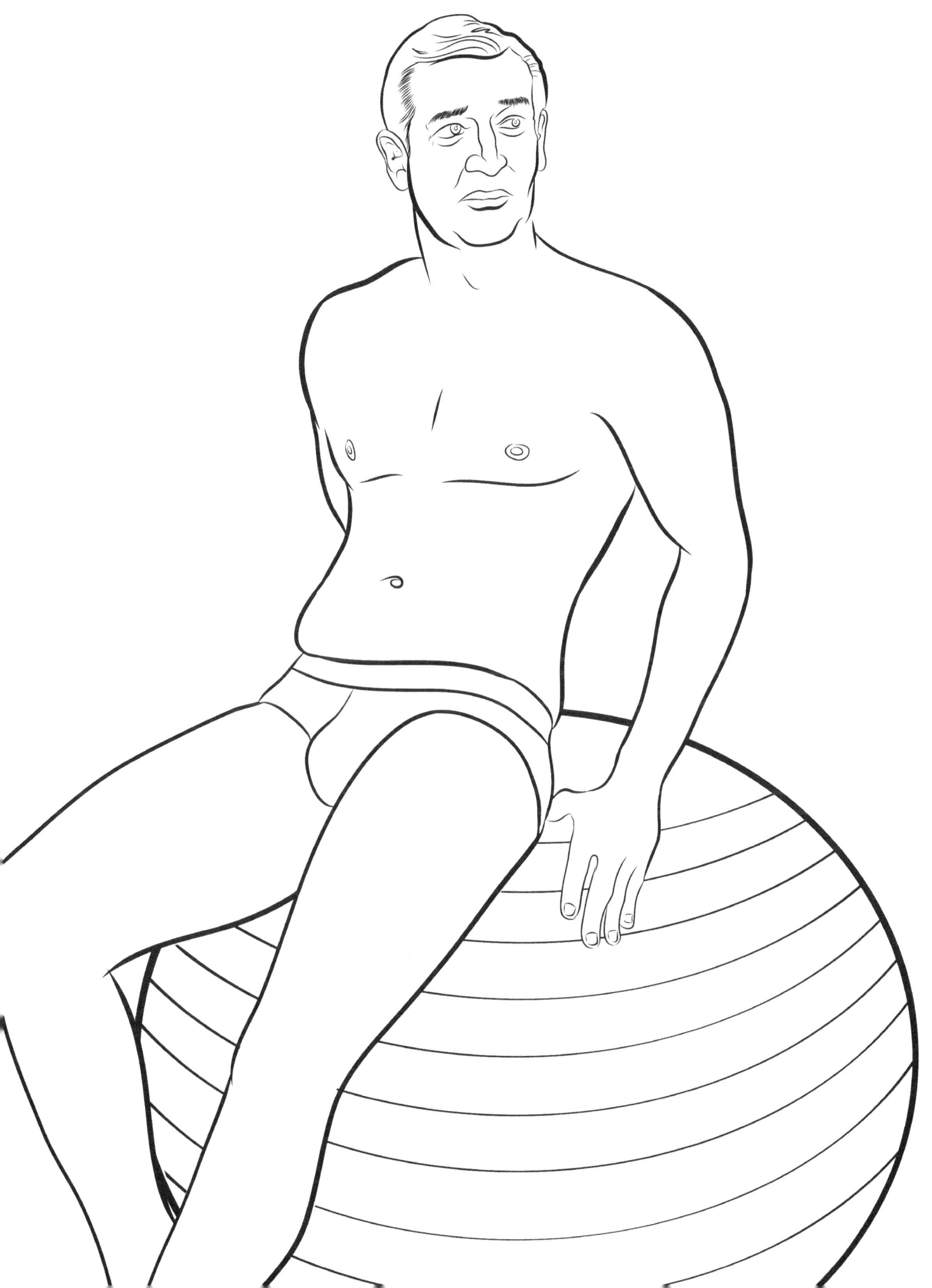

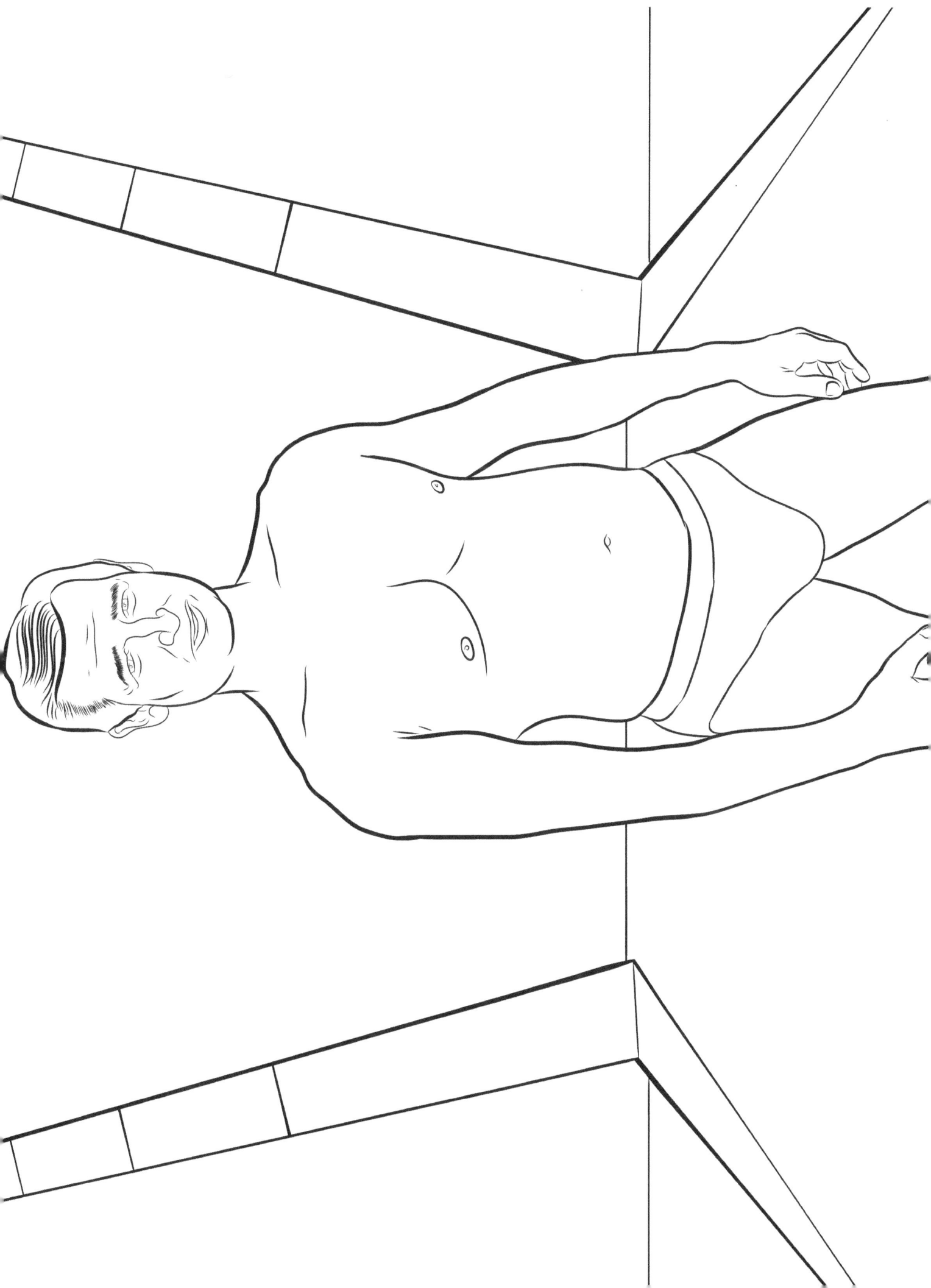

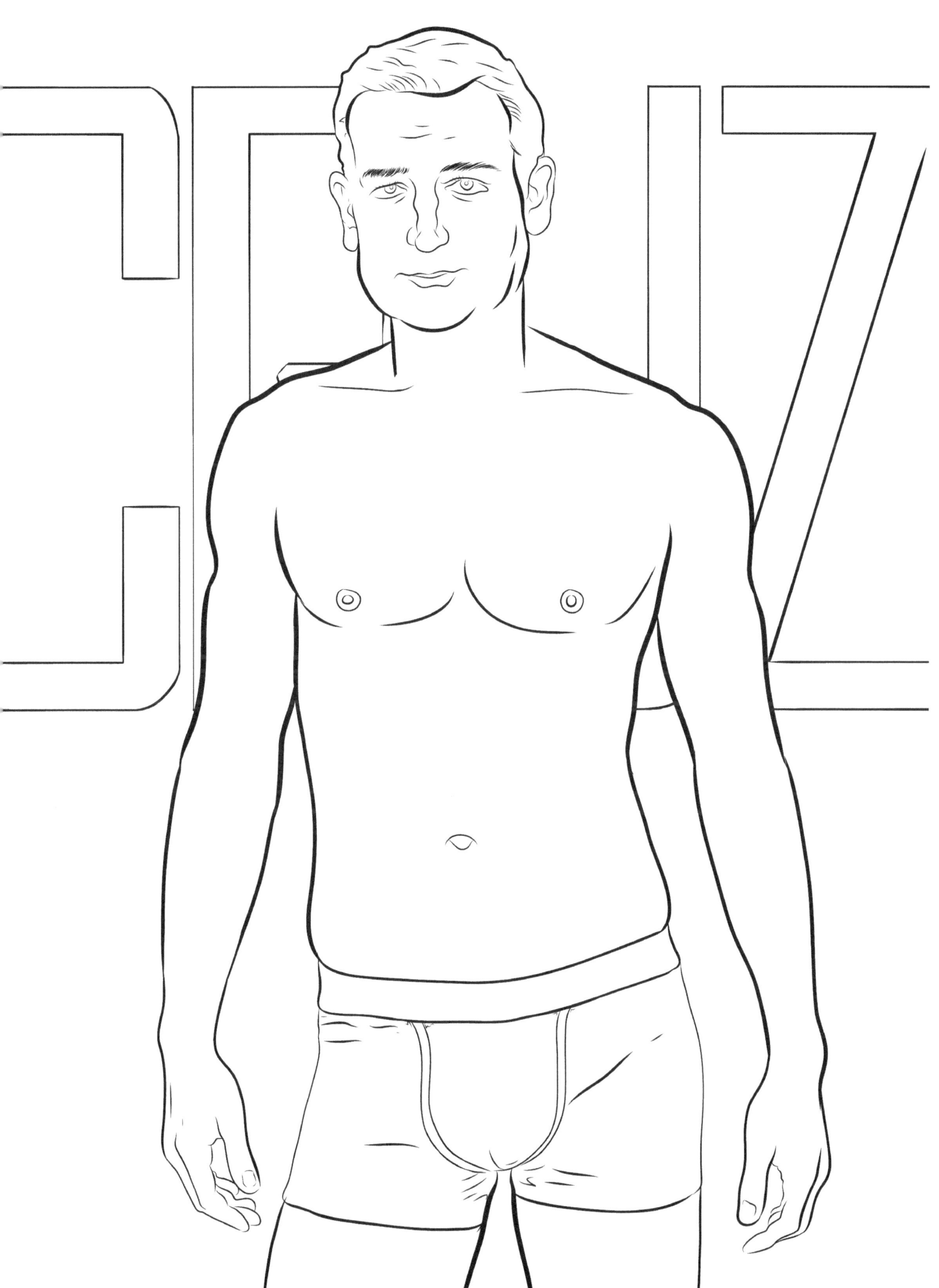

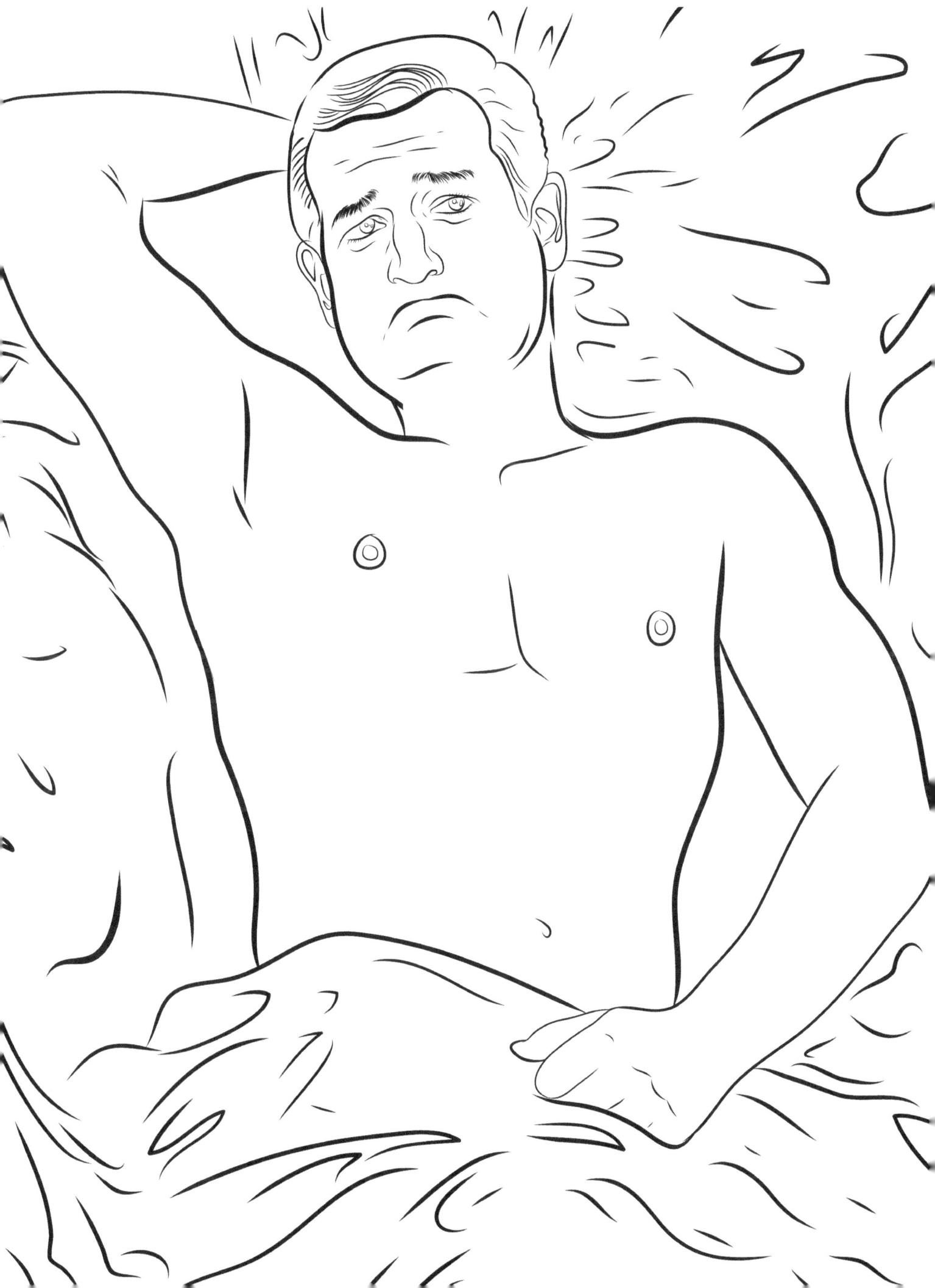

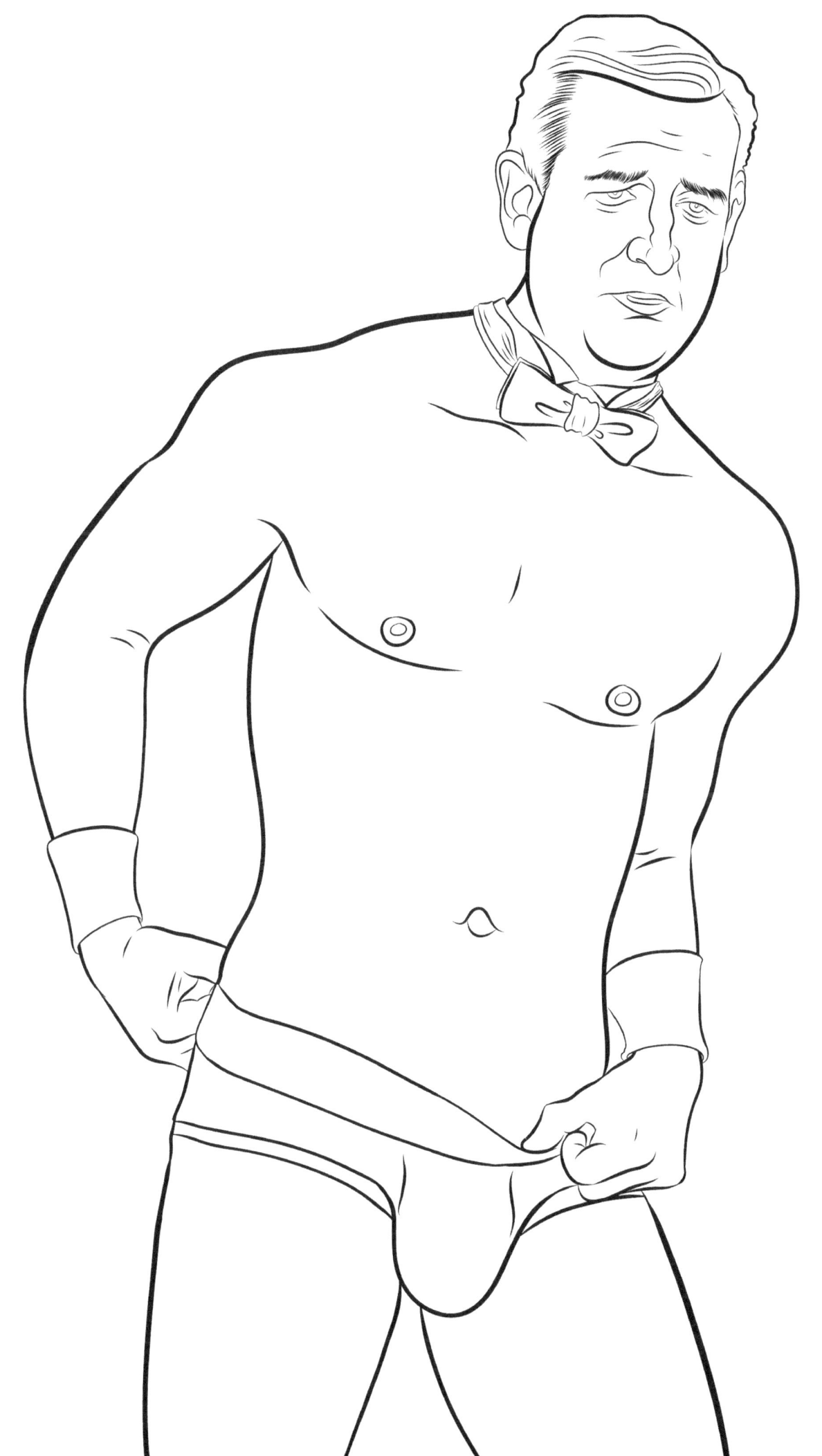

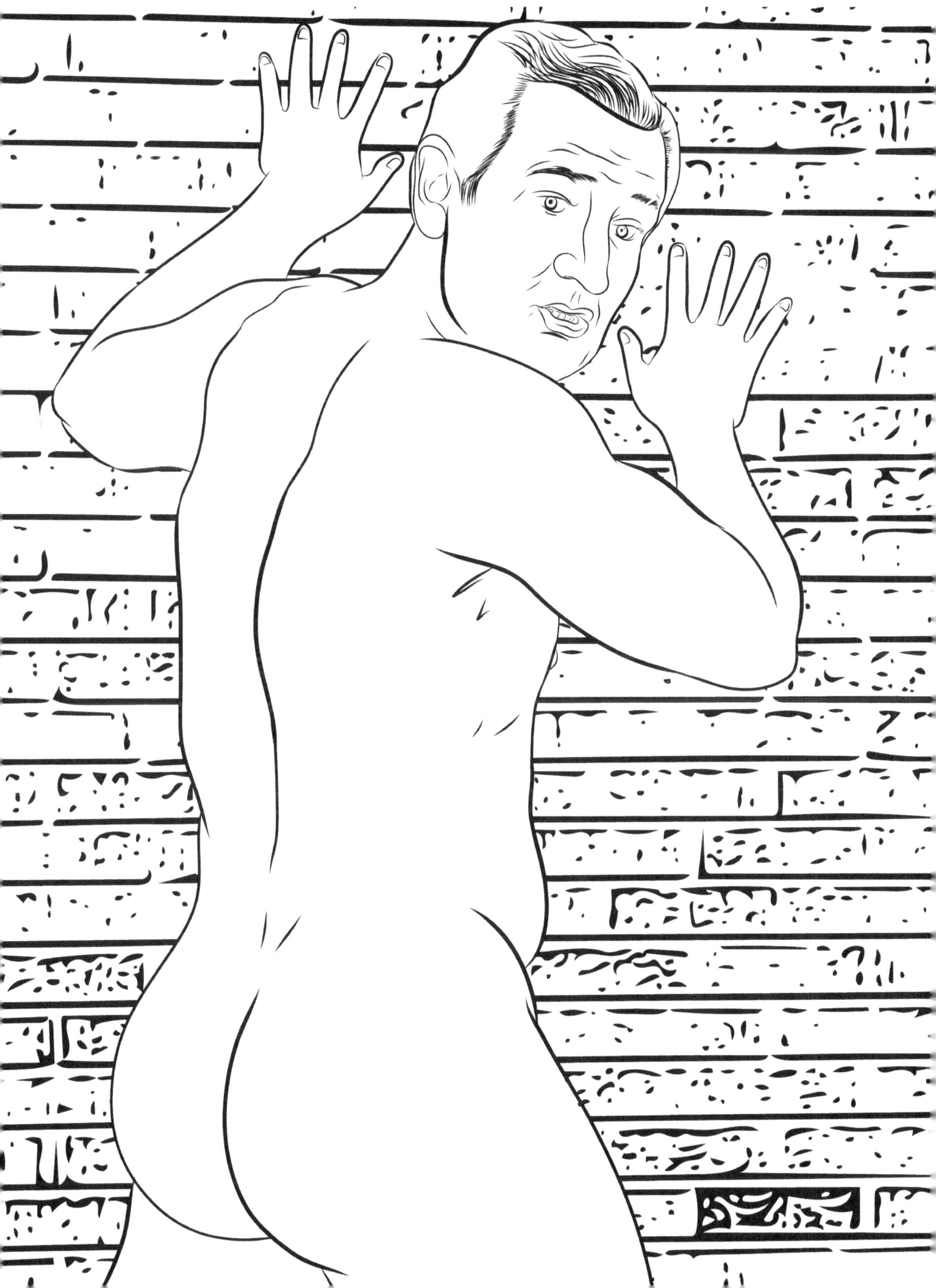

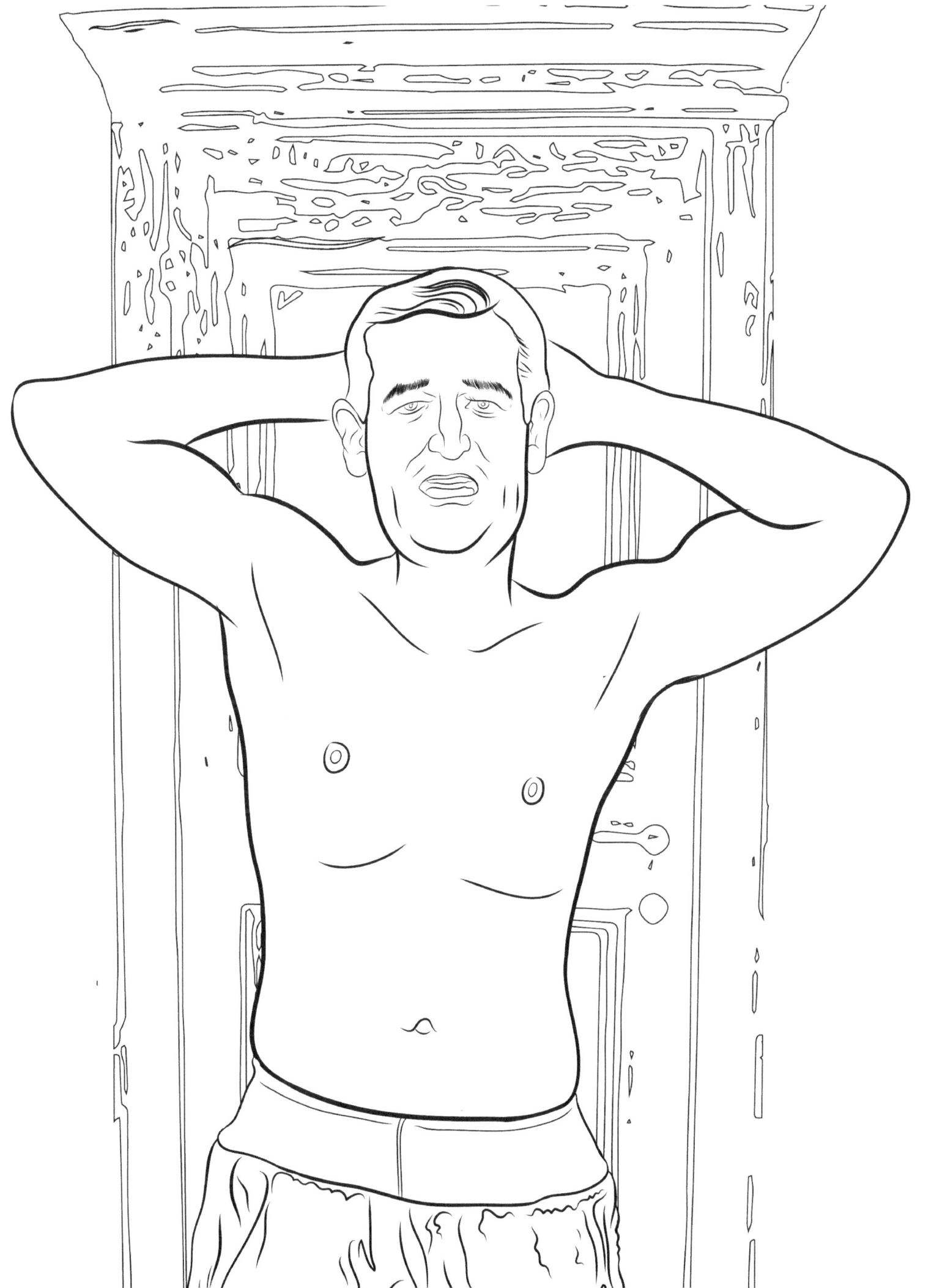

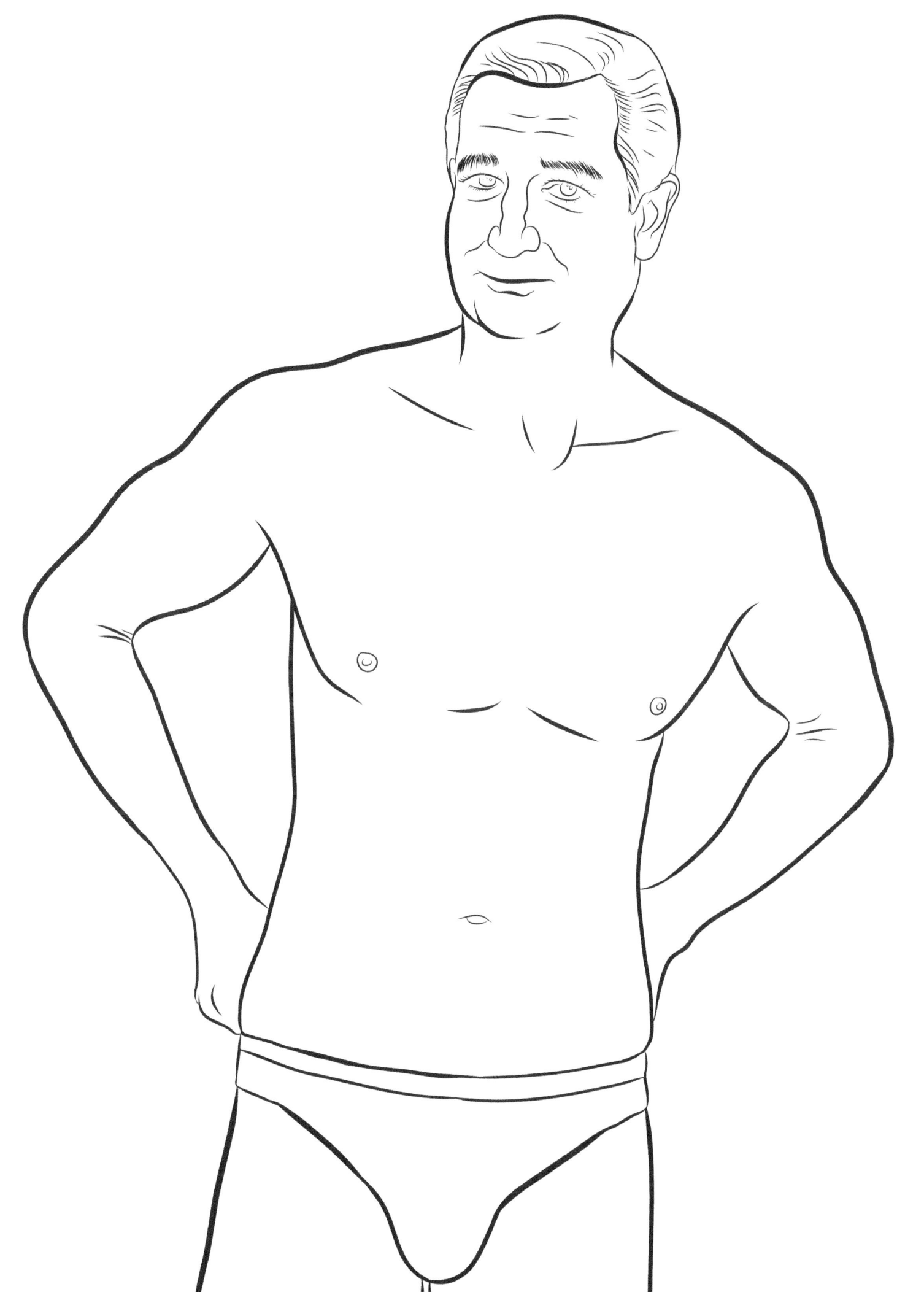

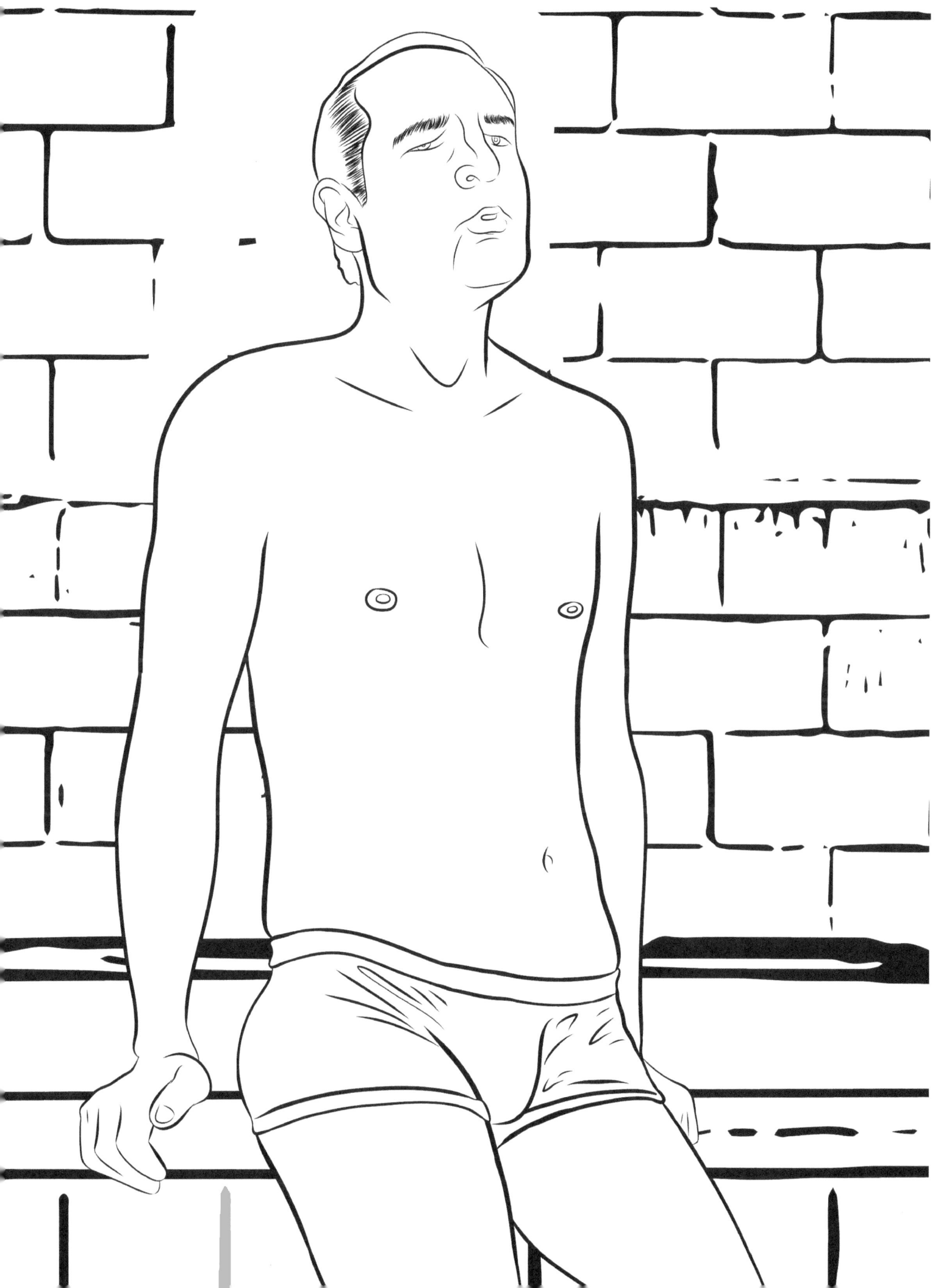

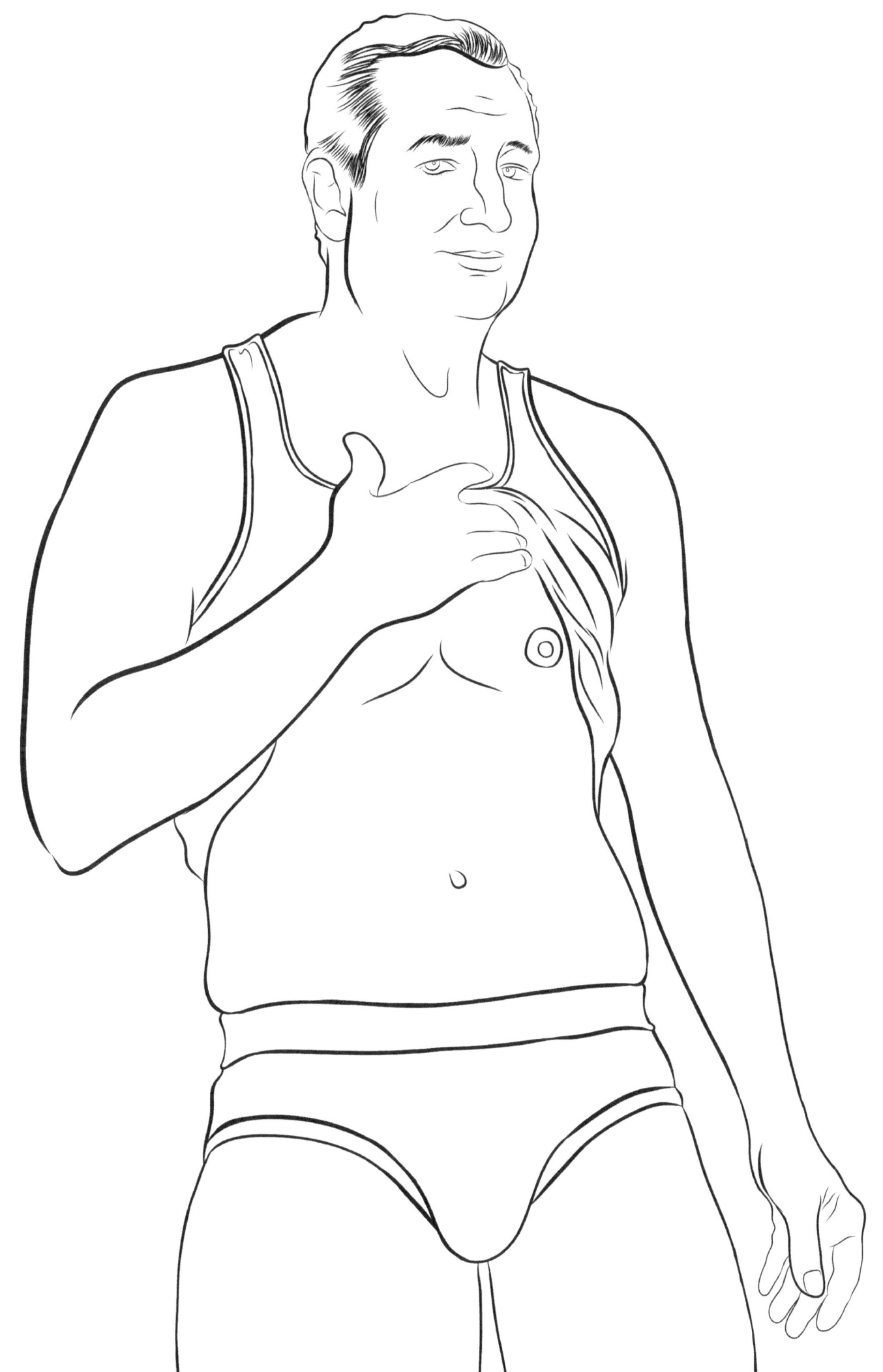

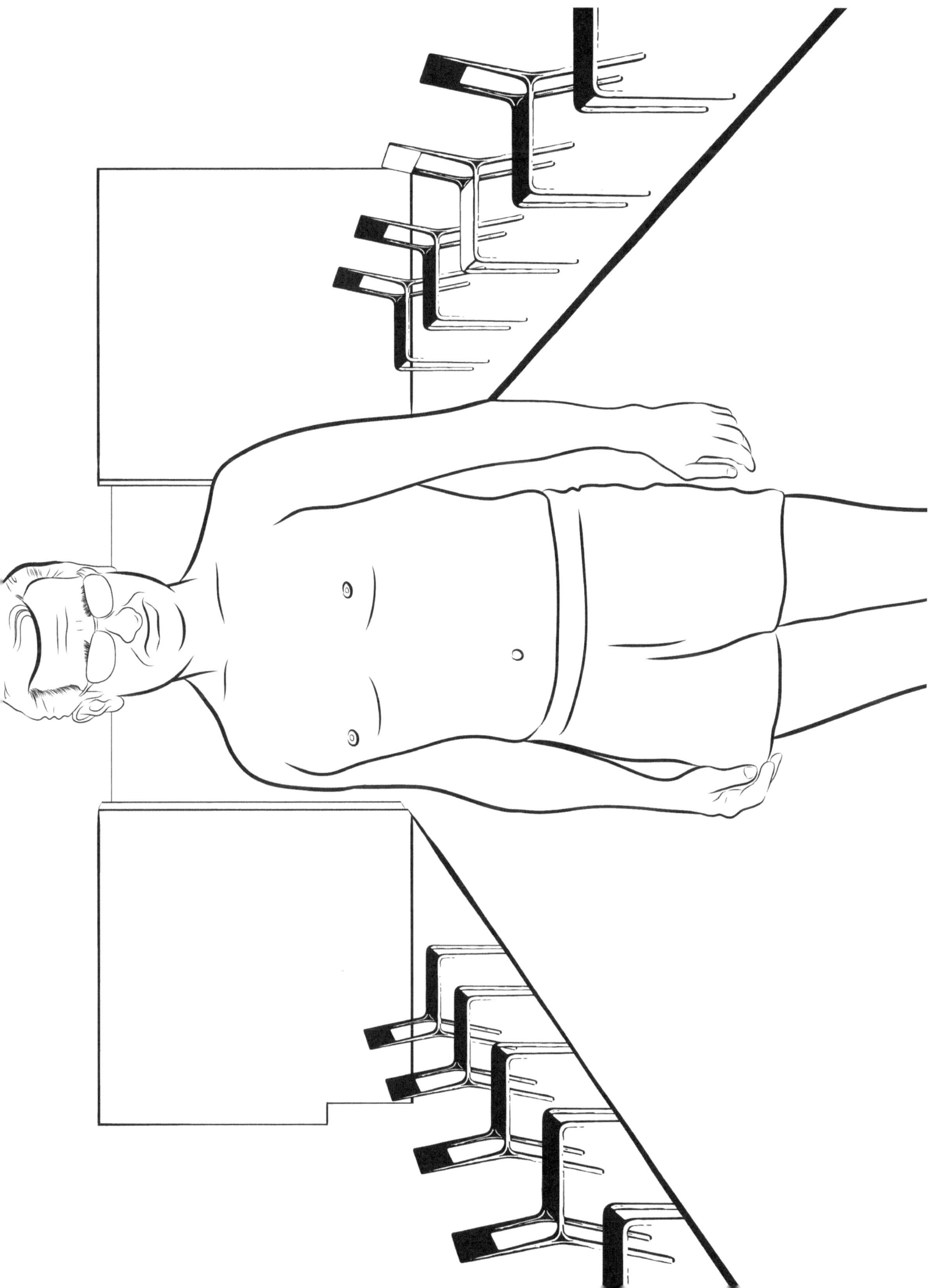

about the author

Rocketship Ace Graphics: exploring life, humor,
and the joy of politics through alcohol & illustration.

this page intentionally left blank

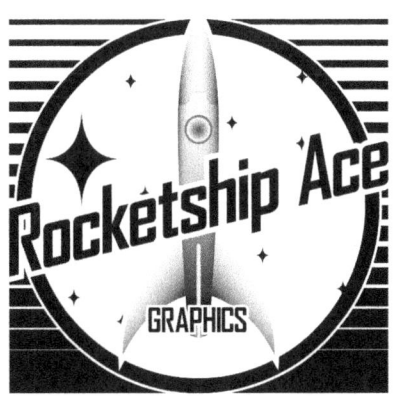